D1449559

ACTIVE SPORTS Kayaking

Published by Creative Education

P.O. Box 227, Mankato, Minnesota 56002

Creative Education is an imprint of The Creative Company

www.thecreativecompany.us

Design by Blue Design

Production by The Design Lab

Printed in the United States of America

Photographs by Alamy (Danita Delimont, Barrie Rokeach), iStockphoto
(Phil Berry, Roberta Casaliggi, Graeme Gilmour, Howard Grill, Gordon
Hunter, Vladimir Ivanov, Lubomir Jendrol, David P. Lewis, Anssi Ruuska,
Christian Sawicki, Jennifer Stone, Michael Walker), SportsChrome
(BONGARTS, Brian Drake, Sport the Library)

Library of Congress Cataloging-in-Publication Data

Bodden, Valerie.

Kayaking / by Valerie Bodden.

p. cm. — (Active sports)

Includes index.

ISBN 978-1-58341-699-0

1. Kayaking—Juvenile literature. I. Title.

GV784.3.B63 2009

797.122'4—dc22   2007051576

First Edition

9 8 7 6 5 4 3 2 1

Kayaking

Valerie Bodden

CREATIVE EDUCATION

You dip your **paddle** into the river. Your boat moves forward. Water sprays your face. Kayaking (*KI-yack-ing*) is exciting!

Kayak paddles are flat on each side.

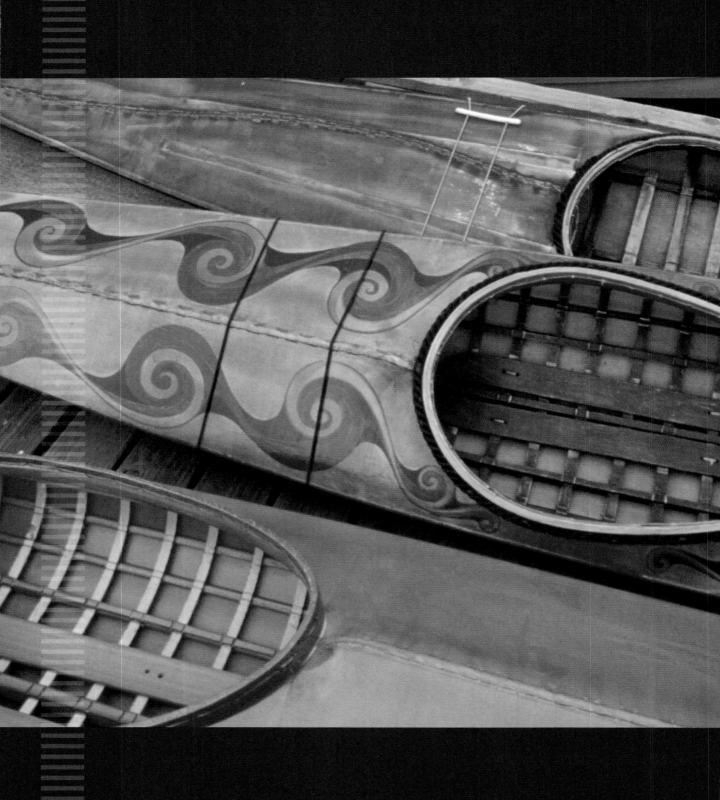

People who kayak through rapids use kayaks that are short and wide.

Kayaks are boats that are usually long and thin. People have been using them for a long time. The first kayaks were built 4,000 to 6,000 years ago. They were used by people who hunted seals and whales. Today, lots of people use kayaks.

Kayakers sit in a hole in the middle of the kayak. Most kayaks are made for one person to sit in at a time. Kayakers use a paddle to pull their boat through the water. They use their paddle to steer, too.

Some kayaks have room to store supplies.

Kayakers have to watch out for big rocks in rapids.

Some people kayak on lakes or **oceans**. Other people kayak down rivers. Some rivers are slow and gentle. But others have lots of rapids. Kayakers have to look ahead at each rapids before going through it. This is called scouting.

Sometimes kayaks tip over. Then kayakers need to swim out of the kayak. Or they can try to turn the kayak back over without getting out. This is called an Eskimo roll.

Sometimes new kayakers practice in a swimming pool!

Slalom (above) and river racing (below) are tough sports.

Some people kayak just for fun. But other people like to race their kayaks. Some kayak races are held on lakes. Other races are on rivers. In slalom (*SLAH-lum*) races, kayakers have to move their boats around poles in the middle of rapids. Some of the best kayakers race in the **Olympics**.

Surf kayakers do tricks on top of ocean waves.

Freestyle kayakers enter contests to do **tricks**. They roll, flip, and bounce their kayaks in the water. Judges decide who does the best tricks. Eric Jackson is a famous freestyle kayaker.

Kayakers have to make sure to stay safe. Kayakers going down rapids need to wear helmets. A helmet protects a kayaker's head from rocks in the water.

Some kayakers like to go over waterfalls!

A spray skirt covers a kayak to keep water out.

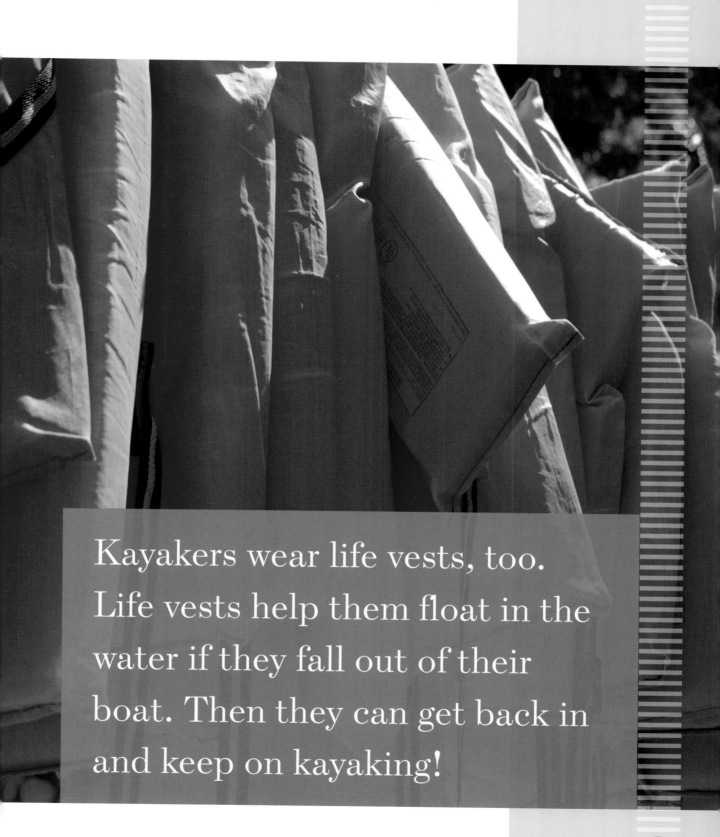

Kayakers wear life vests, too. Life vests help them float in the water if they fall out of their boat. Then they can get back in and keep on kayaking!

People can sit on top of some kayaks.

GLOSSARY

oceans—huge areas of deep, salty water

Olympics—a sports contest for people from around the world; there are lots of different sports included

paddle—a pole with flat ends; a paddle is used to move a boat through water

rapids—a part of a river that moves very fast; it usually passes over rocks

tricks—special moves, such as flips and rolls

INDEX